...and the willow smiled

the poetry of Jacob Moses

"Notice that the stiffest tree is easily cracked, while the bamboo or willow survives by bending with the wind."

-Bruce Lee

Contents

Coniunctio

Within this confined space
Houses enmesh, privacy compromised
Longing for detachment persists
Fading memories of boundaries
Is violation in vogue?
Ecstasy – a novel concept
Wit – a quality maligned
Is fusion an abyss?
Footprints dissolve, life ferments
Beaming obscurity, conjunction coagulated

13th Floor

In Hebrew,
the word for love
numerically corresponds
to 13.

There are 13
positive attributes of God.

Kabbalah teaches us
the transcendence of
the human ego
is represented by 13.

Death in the tarot
is attached to 13.

This represents change;
not literal decomposition
(Just a reminder that tarot's origins are rooted in Kabbalah)

Boys and girls
become men and women
when they get bar and bat mitzvot
at the age of 13.

And while some fear this number
I would not be born without it.
for my grandfather was born on

June 13, 1913.
It was a Friday!

All the positives lacking
from religious zealots
who only associate the number
with witches, demons, and majick
compose the base 13 superstitions
America possesses.

They fail to make the architecture
of our urban infrastructure
stand one story taller.

The Empire State Building
does not have a 13th floor
and those who defend this
have no ground to stand on.

Bestiary

From sound frequencies
blaring through light
creatures roam the terrains
of my subconscious

With a ballpoint
I am the vessel
in which my wildfire
initiates the genesis
of a new world
within a leather bound
graveyard of trees

Images of these beasts
assert dominance
over my non-dominant hand

Intuition guides me to identify
the taxonomy of
my broken sense of clarity

Only to be classified as
a recluse with imaginary friends
in images which would be
unrecognizable to those
far less magical and
significantly less imaginative

These are transmissions
which are sent through me
with the reserved fervor
initiated by the sounds of
Egypt and Tibet
I am the conjurer
who walks a fine line in this
alley of grayness

I am the beast
taking the form of animals
which have long been symbols
of my spiritual DNA

In the truest of forms
this bestiary holds
the broken
and these pages
are the glue

These are the clues
to help me sleuth
how I may be whole
once again

Unsolved Syzygy

Could I just open
Myself to understanding
From a gentle soul?
Nexus forming between us?
Synergy and syzygy?

Is there a connect?
Six eyes linked with visuals?
Whether in plain sight
Or in psychic energies
Bridging eccentricities?

Please solve these riddles
Without force and impatience
Be meticulous
Show me you put in effort
Without rushing this process

No doubt, you can win
Answer questions correctly
Faithful safe cracker
You don't have confirmation
Without my combination

Ode to Pascal's Triangle

With every downward step
There are incremental victories
From numerical order
You embrace rapid succession

Within these three sides expanding
You reach a second dimension
Numbers successively increase
Triangular numbers form

This map of binomial expression
Every story births a new dimension
Triangles become tetrahedrons
Pyramids to the layman

Every generation of a pattern
Born from one singular source
Infinitely strong and growing
Cradled by The One

Fire Bender

Within the darkness
a candle beams

Can I control the flame
I sometimes struggle to control
within my belly?

I see trails of fire
pointing straight

In the divergence of the light
the orange embers
beckon me to follow
every fork in this burning highway

Every exit is a ramp
leading to peace

Fire rests upon my shoulders
when my heart and mind
converge within this meditation

My eyes are the magnet
controlling a compass
fueled by wax

More directions exist
than I had ever fathomed

I can control the altitude
my spirit reaches
and I see heaven emanating
from a candle far from brief

I feel my sense of masculinity
forming as trails denote my chromosomes
on both the x-axis and y-axis

And even when the daylight breaks
this light won't be obscured
for the sun and the moon
within the eyes of the falcon
won't allow the night to perish

Gestalt

According to Google Dictionary
Gestalt is a noun defined as:

an organized whole
that is perceived as more
than the sum of its parts.

This circle underwent shrinkage
and the periphery
is protected by a force field

Can you see a clear picture
of who will stay
and who will equate
friendship with fecklessness?

Over the years
you learn that when your world crumbles
your social life crumbles with you

I can only hope
whomever inherits this earth
knows how to empathize

For the sum of all parts
is knowing the difference
between those who see you as a product
and others who admire your quotients
Intellectual and emotional alike

This inner circle is intact
It is the center of a three-ring circus
where the dead take the spotlight
as minions surround the bodies
from neighboring rings
as the coffin is lowered

Some will reach across to help
Others will simply witness your descent

But at the end of the day…
some of the cords, radii, and diameters
allow you to bounce back
keeping you suspended
as you view the full landscape
your sanctuaries span

Love Poem to Amélie Poulain

Thank you for your gifts
for the city of Paris
needs your wit

Your whimsy
nourishes gardens
succumbing to
droughts and
stubborn weeds

Admittedly I forgot
what drew me to you

If I fathomed a guess
it would be that you are
the human hybrid
of a sparrow and raven

Perhaps your intuition
about the simultaneous
occurrences of
fifteen Parisian orgasms
amused my aura

You are a priestess
who can make garden gnomes
fulfill their destinies

Though you are fictional
your impact is authentic
as budding cherry blossoms
after the winter
ceases to enable
reclusive habits

Kindness is always kismet
as you humbly
improve the lives around you
from inside Café des 2 Moulins

And know that when your mystique
drew love to you
through your webs of riddles
someone would crack your codes
the way you cracked your crème brûlée
and enjoyed its simplicity

All the while
your complexity
was as refreshing
as a reservoir

And I am grateful
you found that
joie de vivre

Terza Rima: Moses

Within your name, I found a legacy
Each letter spells out all our miracles
As Jews, we honor every destiny

You split the waters with a lyrical
combination of a language found
Our bricks for writing are empirical

With fire, you could see the Lord's voice bound
within a bush aiding the Israelites
It tells you how to break through this compound

A stutter never stopped you from the fight
as brother Aaron transcribed with his hand
You left an impact as Jews saw the light

From slavery and from bondage, we all ran
You were excluded for questioning God
and hence did not enter the Promised Land

We are the people who never facade
We are comforted by thy staff and rod

Diamanté: Robins + Crows

robins
spring birth
messenger of peace
birds bridge many realms
from the departed
sent through
crows

Vision Quest

My father's legacy
    exists in Martling's Pond

He offered two catfish
    to the soul of Clove Lakes Park

Whether they survived
    is a mystery to us

But fisherman often spoke
    of their presence in these waters

I remembered biology class
    when I learned how fish spawn

Their offspring contained in eggs
    while fertilized in their nests

One may only hope
    we changed the ecosystem

Perhaps we changed this environment
    with a gift reminiscent of Noah

Twenty years have passed
    since we gave them up

Now their spawn eat the algae
    at the bottom of the pond

Here's hoping future generations
    help habitats harbor harmony

Yet Another Pink Floyd Poem

Using your voice to
speak to a generation
sometimes goes unheard
In the event someone cares
listen if the vibe suits you

Come enjoy the air
Breathing is necessary
when consuming light
from the depths of the cosmos
and the light within your soul

Running away can
only serve to cheat yourself
from felicity
Following like a stalker
are the problems you carry

Synchronicity
sometimes serves to add distress
more than oft needed
Limitations crush the mind
when constrained by Father Time

Death need not be sad
Parts of us must rot away
Consumed by living
are these insecurities
which squatted far too long

Same goes for money
Added pressure to allow
it to consume us
just so we have shelters that
never get inhabited

Now we are at war
Divided among ourselves
in this massacre
against reason and wisdom
and emotion and spirit

So here come the drugs
all those pretty colors spin
as they beckon you
to cross over to this realm
which eliminates your shame

Now you can't think straight
Faulty interface pervades
every single sense
of your rationality
falls quickly by the way side

As the world closes
memories on this journey
are fading to black
for the destination reached
is the dark side of the moon

About the Poet

Jacob Moses (AKA Jack M. Freedman) is a poet and spoken word artist from Staten Island, NY. He previously penned the poetry book, Serotonin Seas (Infinity Publishing, 2005) and edited the poetry anthology, Trails Through the Greenbelt (Infinity Publishing, 2008) . Other projects include the chapbooks Never Lick the Spoon (2015), Tobias (JMF Chapbooks LLC, 2016) and Offerings (co-written by Jared A. Rich and Beth A. Greene) (JMF Chapbooks LLC, 2018).

Jacob has published poetry spanning USA, Canada, UK, France, India, The Netherlands, Ukraine, Thailand, Singapore, and Nigeria. It's as if his poetry is playing a game of Risk. Publications featuring his work include: Third Rail Magazine (2005, 2006), Unquiet Desperation (2007), First Literary Review-East (2011), NYC Voices (2012), espresso ink. (2012), Boston Literary Magazine (2012, 2015), Acoustic Levitation (2012), eunoia review (2012), NYSAI Press (2014, 2017), typoetic-us (2015), POST(blank) (2016), Madness Muse Press (2016), Rat's Ass Review (2016), In Between Hangovers (2016–2017), Free Lit Magazine (2017), Rising Phoenix Review (2017), Anti-Heroin Chic (2017), Quail Bell Magazine (2017), Taj Mahal Review (2017), Whispers (2018), GAMBA Magazine (2018), Anxious Poets Society (2018), STAT®REC (2018), Breadcrumbs Magazine (2018), Ariel Chart (2018), The Sirens Call (2018), ex-ex-lit (2019), Cherry-House Press (2019), Nightingale & Sparrow (2019), Eskimo Pie (2019), CCAR Journal (2019), PPP eZine (2019), ArtHut (2019), and Marías at Sampaguitas (2019).

Jacob has performed at a multitude of venues and was a featured poet at events such as the New York City Poetry Festival, Flame-Con, Brooklyn Wildlife Summer Festival, and The Inspired Word. Venues include Bowery Poetry Club, Nuyorican Poets Cafe, Parkside Lounge, and his old stomping grounds: The Muddy Cup Coffeehouse in Staten

Island. At Muddy Cup, he got his start as a poet and hosted an open mic. September 12, 2002 is his poetry birthday, for a year and a day after 9/11 was too long for him to stay silent.